The Poetry of James K. Baxter

by

J. E. WEIR

WELLINGTON
OXFORD UNIVERSITY PRESS
NEW YORK LONDON MELBOURNE

The Poetry of James K. Baxter

by J. E. Weir

OXFORD UNIVERSITY PRESS, ELY HOUSE, LONDON, W.1
Glasgow New York Toronto Melbourne Wellington
Cape Town Salisbury Ibadan Nairobi Dar es Salaam
Lusaka Addis Ababa Bombay Calcutta Madras Karachi
Lahore Dacca Kuala Lumpur Singapore Hong Kong Tokyo
OXFORD UNIVERSITY PRESS, WALTON HOUSE,
66 GHUZNEE STREET, WELLINGTON.

First published 1970

PRINTED IN NEW ZEALAND BY OTAGO DAILY TIMES, DUNEDIN

CONTENTS

BIOGRAPHICAL

James Keir Baxter was born in Dunedin on the 29th of June, 1926. His father, Archibald Baxter, was a self-educated Otago farmer of Scottish descent who began his life in a sod house on a Scroggs Hill farm. He always retained a lasting love for poetry, and his son has recorded that he 'recited Burns and Shelley and Byron and Blake and Tom Hood and Henry Lawson when the mood took him[1]. . . .'

James Baxter's mother had gained a B.A. degree at Sydney University, and had taken the Tripos in Modern Languages at Newnham College, Cambridge. She was a daughter of Professor J. Macmillan Brown, teacher extraordinary of English and Classics at the University of Canterbury where, it was observed, he became 'a legend for his energy, his prejudices, his utopian writings and works on Pacific ethnology, and his part in shaping the University of New Zealand[2]. . . .'

With such a background it is not surprising, though scarcely inevitable, that the young Baxter should show an early interest in poetry. On this point he remarked:

> Somewhere back in the Freudian fog belt these two strong influences began to work on me. With the same place—the bare coast between Dunedin and Taieri Mouth—and the same people, someone else might have become a prominent Social Creditor and a collector of gold-bearing rocks. But instead I broke out in words[3]. . . .

THE POETRY OF JAMES K. BAXTER

Baxter began to write verse at the age of seven while attending school at Brighton, near Dunedin. He has preserved part of his first poem:

> *O Ocean, in thy rocky bed*
> *The starry fishes swim about—*
> *There coral rocks are strewn around*
> *Like some great temple on the ground*[4]. . . .

The lines are not significant in themselves, but the circumstances of their composition are, for he had climbed into a small opening in a hillside above the sea and there communed with the silence until words emerged. Much later he described the scene of his retreat:

> *. . . a bent cleft*
> *In limestone rock above a pool*
> *Of fluttering scum; bushes to the left,*
> *And an overhang. The passage was dark and cool,*
> *Three yards long perhaps, hidden from any eye*
> *Not acquainted; and the air*
> *Tainted by some odour as if the earth sweated*
> *In primeval sleep. I did nothing there;*
> *There was nothing to do but listen to some greater I*
> *Whose language was silence*[5]. . . .

At the age of nine, Baxter attended the Friends' School on St. John's Hill in Wanganui for a year. Here, as in Otago, he seems to have shared some kind of primitive nature mysticism. There are frequent references to this in his poems; in 'Temple Basin', for instance:

> *The river winding by that altar ground*
> *Where earth's on fire, the birth dance always breaking*
> *Out of the flowering grass, the undead loud*
> *Invisible multitude of the wind horses ranging*
> *From peak to mitred peak, from cloud to tumbling*
> *cloud*[6]. . . .

BIOGRAPHICAL

In 'Virginia Lake':

. . . .

This was the garden and the talking water
Where once a child walked and wondered
At the leaves' treasure house, the brown ducks riding
Over the water face, the four winds calling
His name aloud, and a green world under
Where fish like stars in a fallen heaven glided[7]. . . .

In 'Poem by the Clock Tower, Sumner':

. . . .

Beside the dark sand and the winged foam
Under the shadow of the naked tower
Play the wild children, stranger than Atlanteans.
For them the blazed rock hieroglyph burns clear:
Bear dance and bull dance in the drenched arena
To the sun's trumpet and the waves' crying[8]. . . .

In 1937 he travelled to Europe with his parents and boarded for a time at Sibford School, a Quaker establishment in the Cotswolds—'a pleasant enough place with farms around it, where one could escape at times to disturb the tribes of rooks in the high trees and steal eggs from the farmers' chicken sheds . . .[9].' Some aspects of boarding-school life were not so desirable:

. . . .

Hard to forgive them even now,
Precursors of the adult nightmare—
Franey, Nero of the dormitory,
Holmes, with the habits of a jaguar
And the sleek animal hide,
Waiting in a bend of the high stone stair[10]. . . .

Baxter had not found ease of mind in England or on the Continent where he 'wrote poems, scrapped poems half-begun / On clouds and comets[11]. . . .', nor did his precociousness and extreme sensitivity allow him to settle down contentedly on his return to New Zealand. Yet it was, he claims, his very inability to come to terms with society that led him to poetry, for it was in isolation that he discovered a kind of therapy in verse-making and 'counted it a poor week when I had not written four or five pieces of verse[12]. . . .' He has described himself at this time in his poem 'A Family Photograph 1939':

I, in my fuggy room at the top of the stairs,
A thirteen-year-old schizophrene,
Write poems, wish to die,
And watch the long neat mason-fly
Malignantly serene
Arrive with spiders dopier than my mind
And build his clay dungeons inside the roller blind.[13]

It is clear that his adolescence was a trial of strength with a hostile universe. The conflict was all the more bitter because of his earlier awareness of the joy and innocence of childhood.

On his return from England, Baxter boarded for a further year at the St. John's Hill school in Wanganui. Then he returned to Dunedin and was enrolled at King's High School. It was 1940 and the world was engulfed by war.

Archibald Baxter had undergone considerable suffering in France during the First World War because of his pacifist convictions. Later, in a remarkable book* he had documented his own experiences and those of other conscientious objectors who were forced into the fighting services. In the eighth part of the 'Pig Island Letters' sequence his

---

* *We Will Not Cease;* Victor Gollancz Ltd.. London (1939). Republished (1968) by the Caxton Press, Christchurch, New Zealand.

son has described one of the incidents which helped shape his own later attitudes:

> *When I was only semen in a gland*
> *Or less than that, my father hung*
> *From a torture post at Mud Farm*
> *Because he would not kill. The guards*
> *Fried sausages, and as the snow came darkly*
> *I feared a death by cold in the cold groin*
> *And plotted revolution . . . .*

If the outer world was divided into a militarist majority and a pacifist minority, there were also two different worlds within Baxter's own family. His mother represented academic success, his father, a Scottish semi-tribal tradition. The growing boy must have sensed the difference. He was certainly aware of the hostility of anti-pacifists. He has recorded that members of his family were unable to use a light in the upper room of the house at night for fear that they would be denounced for signalling to Japanese submarines.[14]

At this time, too, he had become vividly aware of the preternatural, a relic, no doubt, of that same sensitivity which led earlier to his nature mysticism and which was to provide him later with a vivid awareness of the supernatural. Of the intermediate phase he wrote:

> *A number of sensational ghost stories which I*
> *read at this time helped to give shape and body*
> *to the subconscious terrors. The one which im-*
> *pressed me most was about a lad who dabbled in*
> *black magic, or something of the sort. At the*
> *end of the story the moralistic narrator observes*
> *him at dusk running and crouching among the*
> *long grass of the churchyard, and finally*
> *scrabbling vainly at the heavy closed door of the*
> *church while large black supernatural dogs drag*

him down. I think it stirred up in my mind the Calvinist image of reprobation. I had only to substitute the auto-erotic practices for black magic, and there I was in the centre of the tale[15]. . . .

Even more significant than these preternatural terrors was the recognition of the sexual instinct at puberty. Baxter's unrelenting criticism of the Calvinist sub-structure of New Zealand society dates from this time when 'All the pressures were on me . . . to accept the Calvinist ethos which underlies our determinedly secular culture like the bones of a dinosaur buried in a suburban garden plot—*work is good; sex is evil; do what you're told, and you'll be all right*[16]. . . .' He has described the period of adolescence as 'the authentic and terrible grey rock desert[17]. . . .' His poem 'Be Happy in Bed' recalls

> *One landscape, many women;*
> *Ambition of that savage empty boy*
> *Haunting the bathing sheds and diamond bay,*
> *Composing verses in an upstairs room*[18]. . . .

'At Day's Bay' also reflects on adolescent grief:

> *. . . I think of*
> *adolescence: that sad boy*
> *I was, thoughts crusted with ice*
> *on the treadmill of self-love,*
>
> *Narcissus damned, who yet brought*
> *like a coal in a hollow*
> *stalk, the seed of fire that runs*
> *through my veins now. I praise that*
> *sad boy now, who having no*
> *hope, did not blow out his brains.*[19]

No other New Zealand writer has expressed as keenly as he the conviction that man inhabits a fallen state.

By the beginning of 1944 Baxter had left King's High School and enrolled at Otago University where his chief interests turned out to be of a non-academic kind: 'Aphrodite, Bacchus and the Holy Spirit were my tutors, but the goddess of good manners and examination passes withheld her smile from me[20].' By the middle of the next year he had decided to break off his studies: 'I thought,' he wrote, 'that I had to find out who I was or else take a large dose of strychnine, and that I needed more elbow room to get on with living and writing[21]. . . .'

Thus from 1945 to 1948 he worked at various labouring jobs in Dunedin and, in that last year, Christchurch, where he also attended occasional lectures at the university. He was employed as a farm worker, a porter in a TB sanitorium, a freezing worker, a foundryman, a postman, a copyholder for a newspaper and a hotel porter. It seems that he would work for a time, drink for a week, and then write poems for just as long as his money held out and he was forced to take another job. During those years of erratic employment the poems in *Blow, Wind of Fruitfulness* were written.

Alcoholism has had few direct effects on Baxter's writing, although, from time to time, it has dictated his choice of subject-matter, as in his 'Lament for Barney Flanagan' where he took an alcoholic as the centrepiece for his picture of fallen and redeemable man. At the same time, there are some indirect effects which one can observe: these are certain qualities of violence, tension and nightmarish imaginings which derive, no doubt, from the haunted perceptions and explosive emotions common among alcoholics.

At the end of 1948 Baxter married and moved to Wellington where he took a job at the Wellington freezing-works and studied Greek History, Art and Literature extramurally from Victoria University. He then worked for a year as a postman before enrolling at Wellington Teachers' Training College and completing his B.A. part-time at the university. After a period of school-teaching he became a sub-editor in the School Publications Branch of the Department of Education but this experience seemed only to crystallize his objections to bureaucracy.

In 1958 he was received into the Roman Catholic Church. Subsequently he wrote:

> *I confess that my own conversion controlled by the Spirit of Love who kindles where he desires to kindle, was founded on the natural ground of that utter lack of credulity, that abyss of scepticism which makes me call myself a modern man. Because I doubted all substantial good, it became possible for me to believe in the Unknown God who is also the son of man*[22]. . . .

In 1962 Baxter resigned from the civil service and became a postman in Wellington. During 1966 and 1967 he moved once again onto the fringe of academic life when he accepted the Robert Burns Fellowship at the University of Otago, a grant which allows a practising writer to work full-time at his craft. When that expired he took part in catechetical work in Dunedin for a year before helping to establish a Narcotics Anonymous group in Auckland in 1969. In 1970 he was living alone at Jerusalem, a tiny settlement up the Wanganui River.

It is necessary to comment on the many minor tragedies which have always been part of Baxter's life. He is quite conscious of these; in fact, he has described his life as having been dogged by a 'sense of grief [which] has attached itself . . . like a tapeworm in the stomach of a polar bear . . . the sense of having been pounded all over with a club by invisible adversaries is generally with me, and has been with me as long as I can remember[23]. . . .'

14

BIOGRAPHICAL

It should not be thought that this is simply the result of misfortune. There is a sense in which any artist will seek out calamities and privations and feed on them. What Baxter seems to have feared most in life was not some inward or outward pain, but the situation of being trapped in domesticity, in normality, in that segment of existence which most people find satisfying. If he has haunted Bohemia it can be only because he has feared that any other mode of existence might choke up in him the double source of fantasy and truth. Thus, in a sense, whatever difficulties he has encountered have been partly chosen by himself. They have given his art substance and are responsible for the tensions which lie at its heart.

POETRY AS MYTH

To claim that poetry is best illuminated by the writer's life is to misunderstand its nature, but because of the particular aesthetic theory which Baxter has adopted, an understanding of his life will help nudge open the door of his verse. The 'I' of Baxter's poems is seldom a fiction (in this he is closer to Lawrence, say, than to Yeats or Eliot). Generally, Baxter speaks through these poems in his own voice, expressing the human condition in terms of his own experience. This practice will be referred to as *mythologising,* a term employed by Baxter himself:

> *An alcoholic grave-robbing friend said to me the other day, as we sat and watched the milkbar cowboys come and go—'I took the wrong turn round the cabbage tree, Jim, a long time ago; and since then I've not been able to change it.' He was mythologising his life; and that's what* **a writer does.** *The trouble is, I can't demythologise it. What happens is either meaningless to me, or else it is mythology*[1]. . . .

He has even constructed a mythology around his own birth:

> *Not too far from the Leith water*
> *My mother saw the mandrake grow*
> *And pulled it. A professor's daughter*
> *She told me some time after how*
> *She had been frightened by a cow*
> *So that the birth-sac broke too soon*

POETRY AS MYTH

And on the twenty-ninth of June
Prematurely I looked at the walls
And yelled[2]. . . .

Baxter has defined a poem as 'a microcosm which contains in symbolic form the known universe of the man who writes it[3]. . . .' and he has suggested that poetry 'presents the crises, violations and reconciliations of the spiritual life in mythical form[4]. . . .' For him, then, the poem is a kind of safety-valve, a way of ordering the chaos of experience; as he has said in 'Pig Island Letters', 'The poem is / A plank laid over the lion's den.'

According to such a conception of the poetic process, two elements must be reconciled: the chaos of human existence laid bare by imagination, feeling and sense faculties, and the discovery of a mythical pattern in the sub-conscious which will provide a pattern of meaning, an ideal image pursued, a shape implicit in the original situation which can be adapted for the purposes of an aesthetic.

This notion of myth-making lies just below the surface of all of Baxter's poetry. In its more formal aspect it is readily identifiable—references to Scandinavian, Latin, Greek, Indian, Polynesian and Biblical mythologies abound in his verse. Sometimes the structure of the poems is swamped by their imposition so that the verse loses coherence and is reduced to a series of multiple images. At its best, however, especially when the poetry is strongly rooted in the New Zealand scene, this practice creates a genuine universality, as in 'The Homecoming':

Odysseus has come home, to the gully farm
Where the macrocarpa windbreak shields a house
Heavy with time's reliques—the brown-filmed
*   photographs*
Of ghosts more real than he; the mankind-measuring
*   arm*

Of a pendulum clock; and true yet to her vows,
His mother, grief's Penelope. At the blind the sea
      wind laughs[5]. . . .

On other occasions the myth is firmly bonded within
the poem by emotional intensity, as in the passage
which describes the destruction of the hive in 'Wild
Bees':

.   .   .   .

O it was Carthage under the Roman torches,
Or loud with flames and falling timber, Troy!
A job well botched. Half of the honey melted
And half the rest young grubs. Through earth-black
      smouldering ashes
And maimed bees groaning, we drew out our plunder.
Little enough their gold, and slight our joy[6]. . . .

Yet even when such easily discernible formal
patterns are not apparent, a mythology (in the sense
of a *schema* of general truth) is still present in his
writing, imposing meaning and order on the chaos
of the events of everyday life.

As a result of this, the *personae* of Baxter's
dramatic poems have sometimes seemed like a
projection of the artist himself rather than a genuine
creation. C. K. Stead has observed that, on occasions,
such poems are illuminated 'with the charge of a
particular emotion which belongs to the poet rather
than to something he has observed in the world
beyond himself'[7]. . . .' In the cases he cites ('Mill
Girl' and 'The Hermit') the criticism is an exact
one, but there are poems ('Seraphion', 'Jack the
Swagger's Song', and 'Ballad of John Silent', for
example) in which the *personae* are successfully
dramatised.

In general it must be admitted that this practice
of mythologising has added a genuine strength to
Baxter's poetry, for by means of a dexterous employ-

ment of myth and archetype he has frequently been able to convey a general truth of human experience accurately observed and movingly recorded.

At the same time, his writing is obstinately personalist. That is why he has had no real imitators, and why his poetry, so varied in style and subject, still manages to convey that distinctive speaking voice. It is *because* he mythologises his life in his verse that the body of his poetry becomes a substitute for an autobiography. The whole of Baxter's life and, therefore, the whole of his writing, represents a search for order.

The title-poems and the first and last poems of his volumes frequently serve as sign-posts to the direction of his thought. In *The Rock Woman*, a representative selection of Baxter's verse,* the first poem, 'Love-Lyric V', concludes:

> *I cannot capture*
> *the mood and mould of the morning*
> *save that it is gauche, yet*
> *graceful: will learn life alas from violence.*

In these terms life is a form of growth to self-knowledge, and art must follow life.

Thus Baxter's verse is the poetry of flux. It represents a search, one requiring violence done to self. That he haunts Bohemia, then, must be, in part at least, because he is afraid of losing contact with that freedom which lies at the heart of life and art.

Between first and last 'The Rock Woman' stands as a central icon, symbol of the breaking-down of self:

> *A rock carved like a woman,*
> *Pain's torso, guardian of the place,*

---

* cf. list of Baxter's publications (p. 80)

Told raining beads. I did not know
What grief her look wrung dry,
In what blind rooms and tombs
I and my fellows would walk heavily . . . .

The conclusion of the search is a hard-won acceptance. The final poem in the collection, 'The Waves', acknowledges this:

.   .   .   .

Wings of the albatross whose shadow
Lies on the seas at noon
I take as the type of a spirit bent
By abstract solitude,
Accepting all . . . .

Then follows that relentlessly truthful conclusion: 'Poems are trash, the flesh I love will die. . . .'

Baxter's poetry records a search for order precisely because this is the personalist verse of a man who kept himself moving, afraid of freezing up, happy to inhabit Bohemia since there one can remain free of those unnecessary restraints that stifle life and art: 'The waves do not debase / Or drown what shares their fluid motion. . . .'

This poetry is clearly written by a man who feels the changing weather in his bones.

THE SEARCH FOR ORDER IN NATURE

It is scarcely surprising that Baxter's first published poems should be concerned with the natural world, for poetic practice in New Zealand at that time was greatly involved with the predicament of Man Alone near the shores and mountains of this 'cold threshold-land'.

Allen Curnow, the most significant poet and critic then active on our literary scene, has formulated this sense of the alienation of Man in a hostile natural environment in terms of a metaphysic: 'The idea that . . . our presence in these islands is accidental, irrelevant; that we are interlopers on an indifferent or hostile scene; that idea, or misgiving, occurs so variously and so often, and in the work of New Zealand poets otherwise so different, that it suggests some common problem of the imagination[1]. . . .'

Curnow viewed this association with islands, the isolation of Man in time and place, as generating a fundamental significance for New Zealand verse: 'Whether open or implicit, it is this vital discovery of self in country and country in self, which gives the best New Zealand verse its character[2]. . . .'

The prevailing literary current undoubtedly had some effect on Baxter's attitudes at this highly impressionable stage of his literary development, but it is possible to exaggerate the extent of his debt to the tradition. The basis of his sense of alienation was really found in his own relationship with society. The hostile universe was a projection of a hostile society, and its disorder was a reflection of his own psychological state. Such an expression of alienation, then, is significantly different from that which Curnow discerned in Baxter's early writing: 'Taking up the theme of our failure to apprehend, imaginatively, the physical realities of land and latitude, Baxter began by interrogating the Otago scene[3]. . . .' The critic has misinterpreted the cause of those morose verses.

As a child Baxter had delighted in the Otago landscape; as an adolescent he had retreated into the earth's sheltering womb to find again that peace which eluded him:

> *. . . Again and again I came*
> *And was healed of the daftness, the demon in the*
>   *head*
> *And the black knot in the thighs, by a silence that*
> *Accepted all[4]. . . .*

The well-loved, comforting natural world that Baxter then knew receded as the pressures of living threatened to overwhelm him.

It should be noted that his attitudes were reinforced by those of the Romantic poets whose verse his father so greatly admired. Their themes exerted a pressure which swung open the gate of Baxter's mind and allowed penetration from the New Zealand environment.

Such was the accumulation of influences that led to those early descriptions of the natural world. Nature, as presented in *Beyond the Palisade*, is the unintelligible goddess, her features foreboding and her ways inimical to human kind. 'The Mountains' illustrates this dark poetic vision:

. . . .

> *The mountains crouch like tigers—or await*
> *As women wait. The mountains have no age.*

But O the heart leaps to behold them loom:

A sense as of vast fate rings in the blood; no refuge,
No refuge is there from the flame that reaches

Among familiar things and makes them seem
Trivial, vain. O spirit walks on the peaks;
Eye glances across a gorge to further crags.
There is no desire: but the stream, but the avalanche
    speaks
And their word is louder than freedom, the mountain
    embrace
Were a death dearer than freedom or freedom's
    flags. . . .

Nature, the savage goddess, entices Man, but he who follows the call 'leaves home, leaves kindred . . . .' In this elemental world there is no room for human freedom, the will is overwhelmed and 'the seeking eyes grow blind . . . .' so that man and nature become one in a meaningless shared existence. The child who once wandered at peace with Nature, the bland nurse, is now trapped in the grasp of the torturer; the fertile garden is distorted into a 'surrealist nightmare' where a 'vast fate' looms.

The poem has Freudian connotations. In his manuscript book Baxter has written 'Mountains are mothers' alongside the poem. The mountains are kindly since their embrace brings 'a death dearer than freedom . . . .'—a final release from the sufferings of adolescence.

It is probably not fanciful to suggest that this animistic conception of the New Zealand landscape also has its roots in the songs of the skalds of the Scandinavian tradition. As a child Baxter had been greatly impressed by his reading of northern mythology. He had, in fact, written a poem which described 'cold Niflheim', world of clouds and shadows, lying in the regions north of the Abyss, and the fountain Hvergelmir, source of the twelve glacial rivers.   The transition from this to the Otago scene where 'giant wings brood over loftily and near . . . .' is readily made.

In the course of this volume Baxter insists on the malignity of nature in these 'lands seen in the light of an inhuman dawn . . . .', in this

> *. . . immense*
> *And hump-backed planet* [*which*] *has cast the slough*
> *Of human habitation*[5]*. . . .*

The philosophy which lies behind these reflections is sometimes nihilistic, always deterministic—his dialogue with nature is commonly an argument about human freedom.   The imagery he uses is often strained and surrealistic.

Blow, Wind of Fruitfulness was published in February, 1948, when Baxter was twenty-one.   Some traces of an animistic conception of the universe remain, but the dominant tone of the collection is lyrical and contrasts markedly with the ponderous verse-forms and doom-laden pronouncements of the poems in *Beyond the Palisade*.

At first glance the general shift in this second collection appears to be towards a theistic interpretation of the universe.   'O Wind Blowing' seems to celebrate this change:

> *O wind blowing from the grave of stars*
> *Wind of dissolution, wind of creation*
> *O breath life-instinct from the lips of God*
> *I am overwhelmed by a truth clear as water*
> *A truth eternal as life is eternal. . .*

It is probable, however, that Baxter is using Jungian concepts rather than Christian ones, that in poems such as this he was entertaining an imaginative conception of the natural world and there encountering something of the divine.

THE SEARCH FOR ORDER IN NATURE

Nature itself or the force, perhaps, behind Nature (the reader faces problems similar to those set by Wordsworth) can bring comfort and tranquillity to the solitary man. This is the theme of that frequently anthologised lyric 'High Country Weather':

> *Alone we are born*
> *And die alone;*
> *Yet see the red-gold cirrus*
> *Over snow-mountain shine.*
>
> *Upon the upland road*
> *Ride easy, stranger:*
> *Surrender to the sky*
> *Your heart of anger.*

Once again, as in childhood, Baxter considers the natural world as the source of peace and order. Whoever contemplates it long enough will share its tranquillity:

> .   .   .   .
>
> *Lie still: let thunder beat upon the brain*
> *Sun clothe the naked shoulders like a grave—*
> *Till air and earth and sea revive again*
> *The mountains and the dark imagined plain*
> *The wild lost city of a mother's love.*[6]

The 'mother' of the last line is Mother Earth, Gea, the mythological figure whom Baxter has celebrated so often in his latest work. She alone can console the natural man.

This last conviction, dating, in all probability, from adolescence, when he used to withdraw into 'the hollow place' to be healed 'by a silence that / Accepted all . . .', has been the foundation of much of Baxter's best verse, verse securely founded in the natural world. 'The Cave' is such a poem:

In a hollow of the fields, where one would least
>   *expect it,*

THE POETRY OF JAMES K. BAXTER

Stark and suddenly this limestone buttress:
A tree whose roots are bound about the stones,
Broad-leaved, hides well that crevice at the base
That leads, one guesses, to the sunless kingdom
Where souls endure the ache of Proserpine.

.   .   .   .

The whole weight of the hill hung over me;
Gladly I would have stayed there and been hidden
From every beast that moves beneath the sun,
From age's enmity and love's contagion. . . .

The lines describe a retreat from a reality which had become too hard to handle. If Baxter had succumbed to the temptation he must surely have formulated a considerable body of exquisite nature verse, so sharp was his ear for the rhythms of earth, but at this very stage his poetry was moving in another direction. 'Haast Pass' can be read on one level as a poem enshrining the myth of isolation in an indifferent universe:

In the dense bush all leaves and bark exude
The odour of mortality; for plants
Accept their death like stones
Rooted for ever in time's torrent bed.

Return from here. We have nothing to learn
From the dank falling of fern spores
Or the pure glacier blaze that melts
Down mountains, flowing to the Tasman.

This earth was never ours. Remember
Rather the tired faces in the pub
The children who have never grown. Return
To the near death, the loves like garden flowers.

Curnow interpreted it in that manner. It does seem, however, that Baxter is announcing a new theme, and that his concern from now on will be Man.

In his first volume Baxter had provided a clue to the likelihood of just such a change. In 'The Mountains' he had written:

. . . .

I will go to the coast-line and mingle with men.
These mountain buttresses build beyond the horizon;
They call: but he whom they lay their spell upon
Leaves home, leaves kindred. . . .

This was one of the points he subsequently made explicit in his critical study *Recent Trends in New Zealand Poetry* (1951). There he referred to the 'dangerous split between the moral and aesthetic factors in art', and noted that the position of the Romantic inclined more nearly to that of the pure aesthete. Of the artist's role he remarked:

> *If he breaks with society and departs into the Wilderness in customary Romantic style, then he loses brotherhood with all but similar outcasts. What Justice demands is something more difficult—that he should remain as a cell of good living in a corrupt society, and in this situation by writing and example attempt to change it. He will thus and only thus escape the isolation of the Romantic*[7]. . .

In 'Haast Pass' Baxter was warning himself of the dangers of Romantic isolation and calling his own attention to 'the tired faces in the pub. . . .' Two other poems in this collection, 'Farmhand' and 'Returned Soldier', indicate the new direction, and a third, 'Sea Noon', contrasts the pleasure arising from the company of men with the menacing countenance of the Nature Goddess.

There is a further change in Baxter's attitude to Nature at this time which is of the first importance.

THE POETRY OF JAMES K. BAXTER

Three poems, 'Let Time Be Still', 'The Track' and 'Tunnel Beach', illustrate a new conviction—that a positive order can be found throughout nature by way of human sexuality.

The Fallen House contains some of Baxter's best-known poems. 'Virginia Lake' is one of these. It views the natural world with the fresh romanticising gaze of a child, and is, in fact, a poem about the lost innocence of childhood:

> *The lake lies blind and glinting in the sun.*
> *Among the reeds the red billed native birds*
> *Step high like dancers. I have found*
> *A tongue to praise them, who was dumb;*
> *And from the deaf morass one word*
> *Breaks with the voices of the numberless*
> *   drowned . . . .*

This is the world where, as a child, Baxter wove his 'mythology of weeds and shells', the real world of a childhood vision—'the leaves' treasure house, the brown ducks riding / Over the water face . . . .' The beauty of that lost world of nature in childhood, that place of order and delight emblematic of innocence, is contrasted with the poet's later state—the legacy of a disordered adolescence, alcoholism and spiritual destitution generally. Such is the grief of the child-man,

> .   .   .   .

> *Who now lies dumb, the black tongue dry*
> *And the eyes weighed with coins.*
> *O out of this rock tomb*
> *Of labyrinthine grief, I start and cry*
> *Toward his real day—the undestroyed*
> *Fantastic Eden of a waking dream.*

One is reminded of Wordsworth's celebration of that primitive world in the 'Immortality Ode' when the universe was apparelled in 'the glory and the freshness of a dream . . .', and of the same writer's sense of loss:

Wither is fled the visionary gleam?
Where is it now, the glory and the dream?

The theme of Wordsworth's great Ode is the key to much of Baxter's writing, for he, too, is concerned with the immortal nature of the human spirit, intuitively known by the child, neglected by the growing man, but recognised again in maturity through intense experience of mind and body.

The third part of *In Fires of No Return* indicates a shift from the Romanticism of the earlier collections towards what can be called the position of the Realist-Romantic. Some of these poems are confused, obsessive, the result of private stresses. Such a confusion exists only in the subjective area of his experience; the outward scene is depicted with a new realistic naturalism.

Baxter's reading of Lawrence Durrell's verse hastened the shift towards realism. This is made clear by the sequence of poems he wrote during his visit to India in 1958, some of which were republished in *Howrah Bridge*. 'Elephanta' shows the new spareness:

.   .   .   .

Great hawks like monoplanes
Above the bony tamarind,

Above the quarried rock sail high, high,
And Shiva like a business uncle watches

The village girls with cans to fill
File through the temple to a covered cistern. . . .

It seems likely that Baxter had come to recognise the dangers of an excessive rhetoric and had determined to pare his verses to the bone.

THE POETRY OF JAMES K. BAXTER

If the style of these poems was changing, the themes remain much the same. 'The Carvers' describes in a foreign setting the therapeutic effect of nature on human lives:

. . . .

> *Look. The wasp has built her nest*
> *Of brown daubed clay below the cornice.*
> *Crabs clinging to the level blocks*
> *With each new shoving wave.*
> *They, the patient carvers*
> *Whose massive music blossomed here*
> *From hewn cloud and blown water,*
> *Ignored the guide's grey chatter*
> *And taught us what to be . . . .*

The 'silence of the daimon' of this poem is demonstrably 'the hollow place', and the voice of earth which 'taught us what to be' is the same as that which spoke at an earlier time, enjoining the high country traveller to 'Surrender to the sky / Your heart of anger.'

Pig Island Letters uses elements of natural description in varying ways. In the tenth section of the title poem Baxter formulates an antidote for old age—a tribal existence spent close to nature,

> *While cloud and green tree like sisters keep*
> *The last door for the natural man . . . .*

Of all the poems in the collection, 'Waipatiki Beach' comes closest to being a nature poem. It contains many of the elements that are best in his later work, a bareness and assurance of form and language, a positive contemplative philosophy, and a strength based on perspectives held in tension—the mythological and the everyday:

> *Under rough kingly walls the black-and-white*
> *Sandpiper treads on stilts the edges*

THE SEARCH FOR ORDER IN NATURE

Of the lagoon, whose cry is like
A creaking door. We came across the ridges

By a bad road, banging in second gear,
Into the only world I love . . . .

There was a time when physical love transformed
the natural world and helped 'to cap and seal my
joy', but now 'bare earth, bare sea' teach a more
lasting lesson, that closer than the union of physical
love is that of death, when flesh, bone and the
probing earth and wave mingle and unite.
A 'lip of sand' left at the gully mouth gives
entrance to the haven of the Earth Mother 'to whom
my poems go / Like ladders down . . . .', bridging
the gap between life and death, bringing order where
it did not previously exist.   There is an oblique
reference here to the tree of Ygdrasil, to whose
roots Odin descended in search of life-giving waters.
The journey does not end there: the protagonist
walks in the company of his son beyond the creek
under its 'froth of floating sticks', beyond the
'hundred-headed cabbage-tree / At the end of the
beach . . .' to 'a bay too small to have a name . . . .'
Only then does he find

Her lion face, the skull-brown Hekate
Ruling my blood since I was born . . . .

Having penetrated outwards in space and inwards
in time, Baxter has completed the mythological
presentation of the event, so that what we are left
with is not so much a nature poem as a parable of
life and death.   What Baxter found in the natural
scene of Waipatiki Beach was an unmistakeable sign
of the presence of death, that event which brings a
final order to the chaos of living.
The natural scene of Baxter's late poems is clearly
the kind of generous wilderness which allows the

growth of the natural man and a tranquil movement towards death. In his poem 'At Day's Bay', as in 'Waipatiki Beach', Baxter codifies nature as the Mother Goddess. The earth is 'Gea's breast, the broad nurse / Who bears with me . . . .' In her lies the harmony of all creation, an aspect of the search for the Lost Eden, since the peace of the natural world reflects that of man in his unfallen state.

Behind this late attitude to nature lies a marked transition from a conception of a malignant natural world to a belief that sexual love can provide an order throughout nature, and finally to the conception of death as the fundamental biological experience. Mother Earth both gives reminders of death and yet provides solace for those journeying towards it. In her care one can rest, as 'The Waves' puts it,

> *Accepted here, here only,*
> *For what one is, not the chalk mask,*
> *Gentility of a robot or a clown,*
> *But the sad mandrake torn*
> *From earth, getting no likely truce*[8]. . . .

What seems to have happened is that Baxter first found a metaphysic which brought order into his own life; subsequently he projected this into his conception of the natural world. Reason, not emotion, has led to the change:

> *. . . The river*
> *is foul weed and sludge*
> *narrower*
> *than I had supposed, fed by*
>
> *a thousand drains: thus*
> *the heart is twisted free*
> *by thought's knife*[9]. . . .

The spare style of this last poem indicates a new

and authentic direction in Baxter's writing and a new sense of detachment towards nature:

> *. . . the creek*
> *runs to sea*
> *finding its way without us.*

THE SEARCH FOR ORDER THROUGH LOVE

There is a dichotomy in Baxter's love poetry which is first discernible in 'Letter to Noel Ginn'. There he describes 'Women as flowers: they are embodiment / Of the gross earth and the rhetorical cloud[1]. . . .' Baxter's early love poems were largely Romantic, but in his later anti-Romantic phase he is much more likely to present womankind as 'embodiment /Of the gross earth . . . .' Yet even as recent a book as *Howrah Bridge* includes poems of both kinds.

One of the earliest references to women in Baxter's published work occurs in 'The Mountains'. It has been remarked that in this poem the mountains symbolise mothers. Yet they do not comfort, they seduce and destroy: 'The mountains crouch like tigers—or await / As women wait . . . .' According to such a frame of reference women are agents of society's plot against the adolescent and against man generally, a point of view adopted increasingly in later poems.

For the greater part, however, these early poems are those of a Romantic vitalist. In 'What Shall We Seek For' love is weighed against power and the 'visionary gleam' of the poet and is judged to be of greater worth:

> . . . .
>
> *Yet could they know, love,*
> *That which we have found;*
> *Could they break free*
> *From the cave of day*

> *Then would be nothing of worth*
> *But life, death, birth,*
> *And the wind-broken ground.*[2]

The verse, unusually good for one writing in his middle 'teens, suggests quite plainly that sexual love provides a meaning for the chaos of existence and a stay from the encroachment of time.

Romantic vitalism is still the prevalent philosophy in *Blow, Wind of Fruitfulness*. 'Let Time Be Still' is a celebratory lyric which envisages a universe ordered by physical love:

.   .   .   .

> *Your mouth was the sun*
> *And green earth under*
> *The rose of your body flowering*
> *Asking and tender*
> *In the timelost season*
> *Of perpetual summer.*

That 'timelost season' is movingly described both in this volume and in *The Fallen House*, and in plotting its course Baxter has written much of his best poetry. 'Tunnel Beach' is a poem of this kind. It demonstrates both Baxter's early Romanticism and its negation:

The waist high sea was rolling
Thunder along her seven iron beaches
When we climbed down to rocks and the curved sand.
Drowned Lyonesse lay lost and tolling
Waiting the cry of the sun's phoenix
From the sea carved cliffs that held us in their hand.

Forgotten there the green
Paddocks we walked an hour before.
The mare and the foal and the witch tormented
    wood

And the flaked salt boughs, for the boughs of flame were seen
Of the first garden and the root
Of graves in your salt mouth and the forehead branded fire . . . .

In the last verse of the poem the 'loud / Voices of the sea's women' prefigure storm, and such a storm, in fact, as can be no longer shut out by the consolations of physical love. Increasingly in Baxter's verse from this time we can trace his abandonment of the staunchly vitalist position. Conversely, he was to come to interpret the sexual relationship as a part of the death experience, and human love as no longer an absolute. What the heart needed was something deeper:

> *. . . the spirit grows*
> *By grieving for the sensual heart in chains.*
> *Birth-pangs that we mistake for burial-pains*
> *Give promise of the everlasting rose*
> *Where bitter Loss consolidates its gains.*
> *This is the answer that no question knows*[3] *. . . .*

The best of the love poems in *The Fallen House* are those which work from a negative frame of reference. One critic has referred to the 'remorseful rhetoric' of such early love poetry[4], and the phrase well describes 'Rocket Show' as it shuffles the antinomies of Romantic love and the cutting-edge of loss:

As warm north rain breaks over suburb houses
Streaming on window glass, its drifting hazes
Covering harbour ranges with a dense hood—
I recall how eighteen months ago I stood
Ankle-deep in sand on an Otago beach
Watching the fireworks flare over strident surf and bach,

THE SEARCH FOR ORDER THROUGH LOVE

In brain grey ash, in heart the seachange flowing
Of one love dying and another growing.

. . . .

*There was little room left where the crowd had
    trampled*
Grass and lupin bare, under the pines that trembled
In gusts from the sea. On a sandhillock I chose
A place to watch from . . . Then the rockets rose
O marvellous, like self-destroying flowers
On slender stems, with seed-pods full of flares
Raining down amber, scarlet, pennies from heaven
On the skyward straining heads and still sea-haven.
*Had they brought death, we would have stood the
    same*
I think, in ecstasy at the world-end flame.

It is the rain streaming reminds me of
Those ardent showers, cathartic love and grief.
*As I walked home through the cold streets by
    moonlight,*
My steps ringing in the October night,
I thought of our strange lives, the grinding cycle
Of death and renewal come to full circle;
And of man's heart, that blind Rosetta stone,
Mad as the polar moon, decipherable by none.

In a review of *The Fallen House* another critic wrote of Baxter's three attitudes to love: 'First there is the Christian track—that we must first love God to make love whole again . . . .', then there is the Hardyesque position 'of stoic recognition and resignation', and finally the Baudelairean which he associates with 'Rocket Show', 'the conclusion that we must go where we are driven by the force of feeling, whether or not we know it is a crippled form of passion which drives and even though we recognise only havoc can come out of it[5]. . . .'

THE POETRY OF JAMES K. BAXTER

The effectiveness of this very fine poem once again depends on perspectives held in tension—the contrasting harmony and disharmony which generate tremendous force within the poem. The brilliant visual imagery of the rockets rising and falling is all the more memorable because of the concrete symbolism by which image and idea are fused in lines of heightened speech that contrast strikingly with the detached, off-hand comment at the close of the verse. The poem ends with a perfectly controlled reflective stanza which is notable for the gravity of its utterance and the severity of the loss which is exposed.

In Fires of No Return shows little or no change from the attitudes of *The Fallen House*. There is, first of all, the Romantic mode which he uses so frequently when writing a poem for his wife.:

    .   .   .   .

> *I sing to the rain's harp, of light renewed,*
> *The black tares broken, fresh the phoenix light*
> *I lost among time's rags and burning tombs.*
>
> *My love walks long in harvest aisles tonight.*[6]

Then there is the attempt at a new realism which informs the third part of this volume; as in 'Letter to the World':

    .   .   .   .

> *The word you want is not the word I give,*
> *I give myself bundled in a word,*
> *The dark figs of sex, the heaven's bird*
> *Hopping and moping in a bone cage.*
> *How, except when he wets his beak with blood*
>   *Can he tell Eden's huge*
> *Indemnity? He moults with lust and rage . . . .*

The mood of these poems approximates that of his sequence from *The Night Shift* (1957) where a dark rhetoric also prevails.* It may be that this reflects his spiritual turmoil at the time, what has been called 'the private phantasmagoria of distress',[7] but whatever the cause, the effect is that of a debased Romanticism.

The wounds of love are another expression of the Fall. Such a 'betrayal in love' gives 'the sense of some almost fatal wound inflicted', an experience which may be common in day-to-day living. 'The particular happening', writes Baxter,

> *. . . a lost lover, a death, some fault of one's own —hardly matters. The point is—at least for a writer's purpose—that he or she recognises inwardly what a child recognises only outwardly —the mystery that theologians have called the Fall of Man. The experience presents a hurdle. Either the writer stops writing; or else writes as if the Fall had not occurred—dead work, sentimental work—or else begins to write truthful poems about the Fall[8] . . . .*

In his review of *In Fires of No Return* C. K. Stead commented on the new mood. He wrote 'the skin of feigned toughness provided by images designed to disgust fails to conceal the weakness within. The poet has offered a distorted image of the world and of his relation to it[9]. . . .' Poems such as 'Letter to the World' emphasise the emotion at the expense of the poetry and seem to have a therapeutic function.

Howrah Bridge offers no new theme, no development which has not already been noted. One finds there admission of an old attraction:

---

* With the exception of 'Pyrrha', Baxter's contributions to *The Night Shift* were written before he turned twenty. Because they were not published until 1957 critics wrongly assumed that they were later work.

.   .   .   .

At night the cages of the past open,
Love shakes the safe dwelling.
Bar the thin door to keep out thieves[10] *....*

'Air Flight to Delhi' reveals that the door is not safe against entry:

.   .   .   .

The old ideograph of peace
Tempted me, with card-playing
On a hard mattress, light between
Bamboo slats. Such love is contraband ....

'The old ideograph of peace' is the Romantic conception of love without suffering. In rejecting the temptation it is obvious that Baxter has moved far from the Romantic vitalism of 'The Track' and 'Let Time Be Still'. Romantic love is illusory and to be rejected; suffering is the one reality and alone brings true self-knowledge.

Passion is still present, but its effects are not nearly as intense as during those earlier years. To some extent this is the natural consequence of age; for the rest, it has followed from spiritual growth, from detachment and from a sense of disillusionment which has led to spiritual adulthood.

The poems of *Pig Island Letters* rehearse much the same attitudes. There is, first of all, a confession of an earlier sexual predilection, as in the third section of the title poem: 'Gripping / A pillow wife in bed / I did my convict drill. . . .', and this helped to teach him the negative wisdom, Loss, since 'It was / Perhaps the winter of beginning . . . .'

Baxter's temperament was of such a kind that the loss was felt most keenly, though he has rationalised the event without pointing to its severity: 'My own natural desire would be for apples, wine and concubines and loud shouting! But no; very quietly one has to accept the Fall and love the fallen; which means to feel in one's bones the process of detachment from life[11]. . . .'

Just as detachment is a manner of dying, so too the sexual liaison embraces the polarities of life and death. And death itself may be merely another way of looking at the lost Eden:

.   .   .   .

In a room where the wind clattered the blind-cord
In the bed of a girl with long plaits
I found the point of entry,
The place where father Adam died[12]. . . .

If the sexual act is a form of dying, it is one of the curious ambivalences of Baxter's writing that its deprivation is also regarded as a death—death in a minor key. The not-yet-dead may be freed from the tensions of active sexuality, but they have not found the ultimate release. This is what is meant by the opening poem in the title sequence:

The gap you speak of—yes, I find it so,
The menopause of the mind. I think of it
As a little death, practising for the greater. . . .

Such an attitude is far removed from the hedonism of 'Tunnel Beach' and 'The Track'. And yet it is, after all, no more than a natural development of his pursuit for 'the lost traveller's dream', 'the uncreated Light'. It is also an aspect of anti-Romanticism:

The terrible phase in any liaison is the point
where the subconscious projections with which
each partner has been willing to clothe the other
cease to be positive; when the figure of the
beloved changes from life-giver, consoler, perfect
friend and mirror, to something else—vampire,

*living corpse, Jack the Ripper, spider woman,
werewolf. It is the negative side of the romantic
equation, firmly repressed at the beginning of
the liaison but likely to come to the surface as
it proceeds*[13]. . . .

A number of poems in this collection are dramatic
narratives which owe something to Robert Lowell.
In such poems as 'Henley Pub', 'Near Kapiti' and
'Great-Uncles and Great-Aunts', Baxter himself
assumes the role of 'erotic fabulist', a term he had
applied to A. D. Hope. In this last poem he assails
the 'temperate love' of the settlers' wives who could
scrub

. . . .

> *all stains from moleskin breeches*
> *except Adam's dirt—and so*
> *the lack ate inwardly like*
> *fire in piled-up couchgrass too*
> *green for it, billowing smoke—*
> *a servant girl's bruised haunches*
>
> *up-ended in the barn, heads*
> *split bloody at the caber-*
> *tossing show—loud pipes, whisky . . .*
> *O Mary, fetch a sugar*
> *bag of snow to freshen my*
> *great-aunts in their burning shrouds.*

In the sixth part of his 'Notes on the Education of
a New Zealand Poet' Baxter explained why human
love became insufficient for him. For twenty years
he had 'fought the wars of Venus, the bitterest of all
to lose'. They are lost because of the complexities of
human nature, because 'each is compelled by the Fall
to regard the loved one as a betrayer or a victim and
judge[14]. . . .'
Perhaps the poem which best expresses the sum of

THE SEARCH FOR ORDER THROUGH LOVE

Baxter's present attitudes to love is 'To Mate With',
a poem as yet (1970) uncollected:

To mate with air is difficult
That sinuous invisible creature
Blows hot, blows cold, rubbing her grit of pollen
On the bodies of ploughmen and mountaineers.

Who itch and curse! To mate with a river
Or a filled-up miner's quarry, that pleases me;
My cold kind mother, Sister Water,
Has no comment, accepts whatever I am,

Yet one may think of tentacles
Reaching, searching from under the darkest ledge,
And not want to be married. To mate with rock
Is obvious, fatal, and what man was made for,

Whose heart of rock trembles like a magnet
For deserts, graves, any hole in the ground
Where he may hide from Zeus. To mate with fire
Is what the young want most, like salamanders

Weeping in solitary flame, embracing
Red-hot stoves, walking the lava crust
An inch away from fire. Then, my old gravedigger,
To mate with a woman is the choice

Containing all other kinds of death—
Fire, water, rock, and the airy succubus,
Without parable, without consolation
Except that each is the other's boulder and victim.[15]

The poem is undoubtedly written 'from the
negative side of the romantic equation', but it has
an added interest, for the guilt is distributed equally
on both man and woman—'each is the other's
boulder and victim': usually the fault is attributed to
the woman.

THE POETRY OF JAMES K. BAXTER

Baxter has now reached a stage of life when the romantic love which features so prominently in his early poems is seen as insufficient. Romantic vitalism was illusory:

> *The hope of the body was coherent love*
> *As if the water sighing on the shores*
> *Would penetrate the hardening muscle, loosen*
> *Whatever had condemned itself in us:*
> *Not the brown flagon, not the lips*
> *Anonymously pressed in the dim light,*
> *But a belief in bodily truth rising*
> *From fountains of Bohemia and the night,*
>
> *The truth behind the lie behind the truth*
> *That Fairburn told us, gaunt*
> *As the great moa, throwing the twisted blunt*
> *Darts in a pub this side of Puhoi—'No*
> *Words make up for what we had in youth.'*
> *For what we did not have: that hunger caught*
> *Each of us, and left us burnt,*
> *Split open, grit-dry, sifting the ash of thought.*[16]

'For what we did not have . . . .': The Romantic has become anti-Romantic; the belief in a life-giving existence through love has given way to a conception of the death-experience ('burnt / Split open, grit-dry . . . .'). The transient relationships described in the earlier love poems were only a temporary stay against the cold flood of time. During those years the implicit hope was for a 'coherent love'.

That 'timelost season / Of perpetual summer' which was the expectation of the Romantic vitalist was, in some ways, illusory. And yet, in other ways, it meant time gained since it provided the right climate for the growth which has brought

> *. . . a belief in bodily truth rising*
> *From fountains of Bohemia and the night . . .*

What he had searched for was 'no earthly attribute' but a glimpse of the 'uncreated Light', the 'everlasting rose'. In the course of his search his poetry has been transmuted from a mere aesthetic civility to a moving statement of valid experience expressed in lines which have the rhythms and energy of life itself.

THE SEARCH FOR ORDER THROUGH RELIGION

The philosophical framework of *Beyond the Palisade* was pre-eminently an adolescent scepticism. Baxter had contemplated the harsh Otago landscape and found no meaning in those

> *. . . mist-hidden walls*
> *Life-moveless where mist moves and asphodel*
> *Lingers, remembers . . .*
>
> *And calls that man and faith should drown*[1]. *. . . .*

The nihilism of these early poems was, however, only a phase, for his energetic mind continued to search for some clue to the nature of reality. 'The Dark Side', from *Poems Unpleasant*, renders quite accurately the successive stages of his early religious development:

> *Horror is learnt early: the child lying*
> *Awake in heavy darkness knows the change*
> *Of thing to daemon, the cupboard ghoul sighing*
> *A hundred epitaphs from midnight to the strange*
> *Malignant dawn—or humpbacked roads will range*
> *At dusk, fearing the rustle of Spiderwitch*
> *Or the ghost howling from the green ditch.*
>
> *Later his mind, a matchstick Hamlet, makes*
> *A verbal barricade, a cold prism*
> *That love alone or the brute nightmare breaks—*
> *Upon the grave of savage animism*
> *He builds that glassy tower not flawed by schism*

That Science loves—like Franklin, from afar
Draws lightning down to fill a Leyden jar.

And yet the fabric frays—so to theology
Turning, he sees the hostile night outside
His lighted window: an antique cosmology
Makes better sense. Thought fails: the grave is wide;
Impassive Chaos claims him as a bride.
He prays, sensing a ghostly enemy,

From Mahu, strangler of souls, sweet Lord preserve
 me.

The poem begins by detailing Baxter's childhood fears which were largely of a preternatural kind. The second stanza describes the adolescent animist of *Beyond the Palisade* merging into the intellectualist of the 'glassy tower . . . that Science loves . . . .' This, in turn, gives way to orthodox religion, Christianity, which itself fails in the face of a bitter reality. All that is left is a bare faith: '*From Mahu, strangler of souls, sweet Lord preserve me.*'

From this point on, it seems probable that suffering and the 'brute nightmare', reality, brought him to a stage where he could hope for a new springtime of religious orthodoxy which might again offer some of those elements of visionary childhood happiness. 'Song for an Old Soak' prays for this:

. . . .

> *Jesus and Mary, make*
> *The springtime come again*
> *Somewhere sometime, or take*
> *The burden of my pain.*
> *I seek the green inn*
> *Where life and death begin.*[2]

Of all the poems in *The Fallen House*, 'The Hermit' expresses most unequivocally the Christian solution to the problems of existence. As he reads his Bible, collects shell-fish from rocky ledges, kneels on a sacking rug in the growing dusk, the hermit is clearly a morality figure. This is, in part, why he does not have the outline of a genuine personality.

Some of the poetry of the third part of *In Fires of No Return* is notable for its extravagant rhetoric:

Stranger beloved, see all weakness cries
In my dark house; rough, importunate
I came to you with false forced praise,
Only for doctor's orders, purges, meat,
A raging beggar hungry for a hand-out.
You gave: I too was sworn to give
The good not mine, the borrowed love.
In my clenched hand it turned to blood and dirt.
No, not in heaven's corridors, but blind
Weeping, deformed, between the sheets of pain
You share our terror, in the secret man
Labour to be[3]. . . .

It has been said that 'such poems . . . do not make comfortable reading . . . .' and that 'the poet here is using shock tactics, in the baroque manner of the Counter-Reformation[4]. . . .' It is, perhaps, more true to say that Baxter has simply lost control of the poem, since the experience behind it, no matter how powerful or genuine, is neither concrete nor coherent. Because of this the energy is meretricious, the images intrusive. 'To God the Son' and related poems fail at the aesthetic level although they remain extremely moving human documents.

But such tortured and self-pitying poems, products of those uncomfortable years in the late 'fifties when it seemed that Baxter might not write well again served another purpose. With the benefit of hindsight we can now say that this was part of the necessary purgation which robbed his life of gentility and his tongue of rhetoric. The movingly honest later poems of *Pig Island Letters* and *The Rock*

Woman would surely never have been written were it not for the struggle with material and spiritual demons.

'The Clown's Coat', from *In Fires of No Return*, is better than other religious poems of the period because of its serenity, its coherence and its relationship with the outward scene:

October: and the whitening pear-tree heaves
Its ignorant beauty at my open door,
Shall this dry branch of knowledge put on leaves
Or soul conceive the summer she was born for?
It may be so; the strong Redeemer's breath
Blows hard upon the ashes of my death. . . .

This is the Christian ethic: that we must die in our mortal natures in order to put on the immortal; that the identification of ourselves with Christ must be complete; that it is this very acceptance of a personal crucifixion in union with the events of Calvary which brings peace to the troubled heart:

. . . .

On them and me the same Face shines.
Lazarus, who was poor, lies safe at home
Beyond the lion's might and starless tomb;
And though the little foxes spoil the vine,
Clown and King, the world's night dumb,
To the same tavern come.

It is interesting to consider that by adopting the basic Christian principles with regard to suffering and abandonment of self Baxter has found a philosophical justification for embracing those tragedies which are necessary to his continuing work as an artist. By not fleeing from the chaos of experience he is able to keep the creative impulse vital and, at the same time, to suffer in union with the Passion of Christ.

THE POETRY OF JAMES K. BAXTER

Religious attitudes are formative to the whole of *Pig Island Letters*. Part three of the title poem is autobiographical and mythologises an event in the life of the boy who

> *. . . saw from the crest of the hill*
> *Pillars of rain move on the dark sea,*
> *A cloud of fire rise up above Japan,*
> *God's body blazing on damnation's tree . . .*

Once again Baxter delineates the Passion as something happening now, not as an event in past time. God suffers in our limbs and we suffer in union with the Cross so that 'no man lives or dies outside the pattern of His Passion[5]. . . .' This belief allows him to maintain his hope for a 'bodily truth rising / From fountains of Bohemia and the night.'

It is almost certainly the sustaining power of his religious convictions that has allowed him to continue living and writing. On 27 May 1949, one year after the publication of *Blow, Wind of Fruitfulness,* Baxter spoke to the Literary Society of Victoria University. His talk was republished under the title 'Why Writers Stop Writing', and reference to it is instructive. Having diagnosed the New Zealand literary scene, he concluded that the output of certain writers had dwindled.

> *partly from fatigue and lack of time, but mainly from their inability to find meaning in a world either dead or disastrous. They required a philosophy which allowed for free will, took on the whole a kindly view of human behaviour (sensual failings in particular), yet recognised irremediable moral conflict[6]. . . .*

His solution was—'orthodox Christianity.'

To some extent the successful rejuvenation of Baxter's poetry in the 'sixties has come about because of the presence of a positive philosophical structure

50

which acts as a retaining-wall within his poems. At the same time there are definite tensions following on 'irremediable moral conflict'. The poetry of *Pig Island Letters* illustrates these two points.

One of the equations which may puzzle a Christian is that of God's Justice and Mercy. In many of Baxter's religious poems the agent of Divine Mercy is the Mother of God, and there can be no doubting the intensity of his Marian devotion.

In the thirteenth and final section of the 'Pig Island Letters' sequence Baxter conducts a dialogue with her. Her person is his theology since she is the moon of mercy reflecting the sun of God's absolute love, and, by the deepest mystery of all, she does not reflect judgment because, being sinless, she was never judged, thus seeing sin in us as not-us and in so doing removing it from us. Such is the argument of the poem.

In her company Baxter is able to recover entrance to that first green garden. Thus it is that in his Marian devotions, in the company of a woman in whom the sexual element does not overtly exist, he has found a source of that innocence for which he has searched life-long. 'To Our Lady of Perpetual Help' proclaims her intercessory powers:

> *Mother, below my life you live,*
> *Nurse of the unlucky ones:*
> *Some old square-headed cabbage-eating priest*
> *Bedragoned by arthritis, or a girl*
> *Who has not found a single trusty man,*
> *All who howl in the rusty frying-pan.*
>
> *Mother, I have no hope unless*
> *You bring me in your holy apron*
> *Clean to the garden gate. Mary, raise*
> *Us who walk the burning slum of days*
> *Not knowing left from right. I praise*
> *Your bar room cross, your star of patience.*[7]

In such a poem as this the complexities of Baxter's theological position are reduced to a simplicity of devotion which must bewilder the secular critic.

In the course of his long search for order in life Baxter has finally embraced a religion which has at its heart a suffering God. In Christianity he has found a dogmatic centre for his awareness of the nature of fallen man; he has also discovered a pledge of renewal. He is now free to acknowledge the love of a woman who represents the mercy of God and also innocence—the loss of which he has so frequently lamented in his best verse.

Baxter's religious poetry has not often been successful. The problem is not peculiarly his, but is one faced by most writers on religious topics and seems to spring from the temptation to write out of a generalised sentiment rather than from a specific event. Baxter's religious poetry is most successful when it is written in close conjunction with the natural scene (e.g., the magnificent 'Poem in the Matukituki Valley'), or when it helps define his attitudes towards society.

Orthodox Christianity has given Baxter much more than a store of themes and images. By adopting it he has inherited 'a philosophy which [allows] for free will, [takes] on the whole a kindly view of human behaviour (sensual failings in particular), yet [which recognises] irremediable moral conflict . . . .'

It is this discovery which has allowed 'that sad boy' to continue living and writing. In Christianity he has discovered a pattern of meaning through loss and suffering, a new order for life itself; and in his religious poetry, more especially when it affirms the antithesis of the real and the ideal in retrospective terms, Baxter enriches our conception of the human condition with a genuine vision of life presented *sub specie aeternitatis.*

THE SEARCH FOR ORDER IN SOCIETY

At a surprisingly early stage in his writing Baxter entered the lists against certain attitudes prevalent in our society. It will be remembered that he had written 'If he [the poet] breaks with society and departs into the wilderness in customary Romantic style, then he loses brotherhood with all but similar outcasts . . . .' Instead he had concluded that the artist is obliged to remain 'as a cell of good living in a corrupt society, and in this situation by writing and example [to] attempt to change it[1]. . . .'

Baxter's varied attacks on social ills are directed especially against the evil trinity of monotony, anarchy and atrocity which so bedevil contemporary living. Again and again in his verse we encounter the urgent, hortatory voice of the social critic. At times the writing remains that of the publicist, but on other occasions his undoubted sincerity merges with the skill of a considerable artist to produce works as moving as 'On Reading Yevtushenko'.

Baxter attributes the montony of life to a secular residual puritanism, to the fact that our society is no longer theocentric, and to our failure to recognise that we inhabit a post-lapsarian condition. This last is 'the second curse, the man-made one . . . the falsifying and sterilising of life by a civilisation that tries to pretend there never was a Fall: it is the curse of emotional and intellectual blindness[2]. . . .' That, he maintains, accounts for our lack of pity for those who bear the marks of the Fall in body or spirit, and explains our inability to rejoice in a subsequent salvation. Once pity and pleasure are gone, we are left with only a residual life—'the joy-killing fabric of our secular society[3]. . . .', the kind of life endured by the inhabitants of 'Calvary Street' who inevitably fail to communicate with one another.

The charge is advanced in 'Green Figs at Table':

> *. . . Society as undertaker*
> *Measures us for coffins, plugs up the orifices*
> *By which pleasure might enter or pity escape[4]. . . .*

Our patron is 'Sisyphus', that

> *. . . . .*
>
> *Mechanic of an old fraternity*
> *To whom the simple and unchanging*
> *Processes of day and night*
> *Seem but a cage, a treadmill motion[5]. . . .*

In a poem dedicated to Louis Johnson he makes the point once again:

> *'The icy dawn of the 'sixties'—*
> *Yes, you have it there.*
> *Today I saw a black sperm whale*
> *Rolled on the rocks at Pukerua Bay*
>
> *. . . . .*
>
> *Under the sunset fires it seemed to be*
> *The body of our common love*
> *That bedrooms, bar rooms never killed,*
> *The natural power behind our acts and verses*
> *Murdered by triviality.[6]*

Most plainly of all, 'The Fear of Change' blames us for 'the falsifying and sterilising of life . . . .':

> *If you and I were woken suddenly*
> *By the drums of revolution in the street—*
> *Or suppose the door shot open, and there stood*
> *Upright and singing a young bullfighter*

With a skin of rough wine, offering to each of us
Death, sex, hope—or even just an
Earthquake, making the trees thrash, the roofs tumble
Calling us loudly to consider God—

Let us admit with no shame whatever,
We are not that kind of people:
We have learnt to weigh each word like an ounce
*   of butter;*
Our talent is for anger and monotony—

Therefore we will survive the singers,
The fighters, the so-called lovers—we will bury them
Regretfully, and spend a whole wet Sunday
Arguing whether the corpses were dressed in black
*   or red.*[7]

Baxter's strictures against the monotony of New
Zealand society are often so strongly phrased that it
does not surprise to find that his affinities seem to lie
rather with the dead than with the living:

. . . .

But I am friendlier with those Puritans,
The dead who rot on single beds

Of concrete where the steam-vents rise,
Beyond misapprehension, drugs, and those

Demons of lucre and great boredom
The living cannot exorcise[8]. . . .

If the puritan ethic has contributed greatly to the
monotony of modern living, as Baxter believes, it is
because it has affected our approach to education,
work, recreation. Of all the contributory elements
to a national puritanism it is possible to select only
one for consideration.

Baxter's jousting with the method of education in
this country can be traced back as far as *Blow, Wind*

of Fruitfulness. In 'Envoi' he described the university scene:

> *Attenuate ghosts expound their lean*
> *Philosophies of When and If;*
> *And oft on that enchanted green*
> *Chimera mates with hippogriff.*
>
> *The classics student feels an urge*
> *To emulate Empedocles*
> *But rides upon the lava surge—*
> *Oh forest of the bloody trees—*
>
> Per ardua ad astra: *blind*
> *Inscription from a catacomb.*
> Lost, one original heart and mind
> *Between the pub and lecture-room.*

He himself refused to allow the educative process to affect him greatly: 'As soon as it came near me, I instinctively slipped my mind into neutral, became passive, inert, allowed myself to be pushed around to a state of suspended animation[9]. . . .' Only in this way, if unconsciously, was it possible for the artist to protect that deposit of original knowledge which should be his most prized possession: 'I was unconsciously erecting my defences around that core of primitive experience, that ineducable self which I like to call a dinosaur's egg . . . .' Our educational process is likely to injure this: 'Unfortunately the abstract analytical processes which the schools were able to offer me . . . have the side-effect of neutralising this kind of experience and making it inaccessible to the conscious mind . . . .'

He has rationalised from that early intuition: 'There are two types of learning which seem to be mutually exclusive—the first being the discovery of a sacred pattern in natural events; the second the acquisition of the lens of abstract thought, which sees nothing sacred in heaven or on middle earth . . . .'. His conclusion is that our pattern of education should be a voluntary one, and one, moreover, that allows for natural contemplation. But this will not eventuate for our technological age does not want such an end-product of the educational system. Rather, because '. . . our firms and departments require literate peons for their dreary empires of economic liberalism . . . we have universal and compulsory education . . . .'

Even the universities have come under fire. Earlier he had found that his years of casual manual work had not been 'conducive to / The exercise of one's imagination . . . .' so that he had been obliged once again to associate with 'the academic crew / Whom I despised for undue cerebration / That leads to withering of the heart and thew[10] . . . .', a condition he describes in his epigram 'On a University Critic':

> *Urbanus fears I'm lunatic*
> *Through women, grog and popery,*
> *Teetotal, celibate, agnostic*
> *Urbanus cultivates his barren fig tree.*[11]

He has further criticised the universities because of their association with the bureaucracy, 'the administrative machines which act out the fantasies of the dull, man-killing brain of Caesar[12] . . .', and he has persisted with his criticisms of university life despite his several associations with it. 'Letter to Robert Burns' describes his own resistance to learning:

> *King Robert, on your anvil stone*
> *Above the lumbering Octagon*
> *To you I raise a brother's horn*
> *Led by the wandering unicorn*
> *Of total insecurity.*
> *Never let your dead eye look*

THE POETRY OF JAMES K. BAXTER

Up from Highland Mary's book
To the fat scrag-end of the Varsity.

Kilmarnock hag and dominie
Watch there the grey Leith water drum
With laughter from a bird's beak
At what their learning has left out.
They tried to make my devil speak
With the iron boot of education
(Psychology, French, Latin)—
But though they drove the wedges in
Till the blood and marrow spouted out,
That spirit was dumb[13]. . . .

If education is one of the factors which has led
to the monotony of our social scene, we may con-
clude that in attacking both the cause and its effect
Baxter is trying to do two things: to preserve a
deliberately-willed chaos in life which he can order
in his art, and to keep a clear eye on the sacredness
of life itself.

He has suggested a less formal kind of education
which would do these things. He would have pre-
ferred to have remained

> *till ten year old, on a farm in the South Island*
> *mountains or the Urewera country, learning to*
> *handle a horse and a dog and a gun; then, for*
> *a year or two, during puberty, in a Maori pa;*
> *then perhaps on the coastal boats. By now I*
> *might have owned a good fishing launch. One*
> *could still have learned to read and write. There*
> *is no lack of libraries in this country*[14]. . . .

The second element of an evil trinity which Baxter
has diagnosed as afflicting our society is what he
terms 'anarchy', a word which must be interpreted
in a very broad sense as in Yeats's 'The Second
Coming', where it seems to imply man's loss of

contact with a sustaining, underlying reality. As Baxter uses it, the term also includes society's failure to recognise the moral law of personal freedom and the lack of genuine love which follows on that.

His political and economic sympathies seem to be socialist yet he is also well aware that socialism multiplies the forms of organisation and administration in many areas of life, thus restricting the subject's liberty of action and making it difficult for him to exercise a personal responsibility or to affirm his personality. Baxter illustrates this point in the eighth section of the 'Pig Island Letters' sequence when he reflects on the punishment his father underwent for refusing to fight in the First World War:

> . . . . *His black and swollen thumbs*
> *Explained the brotherhood of man,*
>
> *But he is old now in his apple garden*
> *And we have seen our strong Antaeus die*
> *In the glass castle of the bureaucracies*
> *Robbing our bread of salt. Shall Marx and Christ*
> *Share beds this side of Jordan? I set now*
> *Unwillingly these words down:*
>
> Political action in its source is pure,
> Human, direct, but in its civil function
> Becomes the jail it laboured to destroy.

The result of a failure to recognise personal freedom is a failure to love. In this context Baxter has often argued aggressively in the columns of the daily papers and in periodicals opposing such things as economic liberalism and society's lack of understanding for alcoholics, homosexuals and juvenile delinquents. He defends, in fact, with charity and sympathy, all those whom the puritan ethic would condemn.

THE POETRY OF JAMES K. BAXTER

It may well be that his own experiences as an adolescent and during the years following have led to his great sympathy for the social non-conformist. What happened to him during those unhappy years in Dunedin, Christchurch and Wellington taught him the need for love and understanding and the dangers of that legalism which is an aspect of anarchy in its broadest sense.

The third tragedy which Baxter has distinguished as a feature of the contemporary scene is atrocity. Under this heading can be included his condemnations of racialism, imperialism, totalitarianism and, of course, militarism.

None of Baxter's anti-war poetry is particularly good. Such pieces as 'A Bucket of Blood for a Dollar', 'The Green Beret', 'The Gunner's Lament' and 'a death song for mr mouldybroke' are a simple kind of verse intended for circulation among a wide reading-public. All four poems were, in fact, published in broadsheet form. Their tone is journalistic, as in the first-named:

> *'You'll have to learn,' said Uncle Sam*
> *'The Yankee way of work*
> *Now that you've joined in our crusade*
> *Against the modern Turk;*
> *The capital of the commonwealth is*
> *Not London, but New York.'*
>
> *'Don't tell them that,' cried Holyoake,*
> *'In Thames or Dannevirke.'*[15] . . . .

It is in 'a death song for mr mouldybroke' that the intensity of Baxter's anti-militarism best survives:

.　　.　　.　　.　　.　　.　　.　　.　　.

when the death bomb fell on nagasaki
some of the people were going to mass
it didn't stop them from having their skins
peeled off like stockings by the big bright flash . . . .

THE SEARCH FOR ORDER IN SOCIETY

Both this poem and the eighth section of the 'Pig Island Letters' sequence reveal that when he is writing on such topics he tends to subordinate everything else to his subject, and that much of his material is not assimilated into the poetry. The failing may be inherent in the very attitude he has adopted, for in his campaign against the monotony, anarchy and atrocity which mar our world he has tried to remain faithful to that position which he stipulated as necessary for the artist in *Recent Trends in New Zealand Poetry*—'to remain as a cell of good living in a corrupt society, and in this situation by writing and example [to] attempt to change it . . . .' His social verse has been written in an attempt at furthering a new order in society.

Very often he has used the ballad form as his vehicle for social statement as in his 'Lament for Barney Flanagan' and 'Calvary Street'. His strictures against society can thus be formulated in simple, lively terms. The form also helps to protect his writing from the sententiousness to which it might otherwise incline.

Often the tone of his social poetry is too strident, but when he writes with a quiet lyricism on remembered events of his own experience and using the natural world for his symbols, he can achieve a poignancy which validates his criticism:

When the mine exploded at Kaitangata
Trucks flew out as if from the barrel of a gun,
Trucks and truckers, bodies of men,
Or so my father told me;
       and far down
In those dark passages they heard faintly
The waves of the sea hammer
Above their heads.
       My father's hands are corded
With swollen veins, but my hands are thinner

And my thoughts are cold, Zhenya Yevtushenko;
They are covered with black dust.
        Reading you
I remember our own strangled Revolution:
1935. The body of our Adam was dismembered
By statisticians.
        I would like to meet you
Quietly in a café, where hoboes and freckled girls
Drink, talk; not to pump you; only to revalue in your
   company
Explosions, waves of the sea.[16]

Undoubtedly Baxter's poetry has sometimes suffered as a result of his social preoccupations (although this would obviously not trouble him in the least). At the same time, these have added a breadth of vision, a humanitarianism and an honest analysis of the human condition without which we would be much the poorer.

THE POETRY OF LOSS AND THE SEARCH FOR EDEN

There is a sense in which the words 'poetry of loss' apply to almost all that Baxter has written, for much of his poetry relies on an adaptation of the Tudor antithesis of the mutable and the ideal, but the term will be restricted here to those poems in which he laments the lost innocence of childhood.

It is in 'Christmas Poem' from *Blow, Wind of Fruitfulness* that Baxter first uses the technique of the child-observer and contrasts his later grief with the idyllic happiness of childhood:

.   .   .   .

> *I remember the roses of*
> *A childhood garden,*
> *And the first eyes of grief*
> *For flowers that redden*
> *Yet rot in garden mould.*
> *Our lives cannot be filled*
> *By labour or love*
> *All days and always strong—*
> *Wind weights the sky and singing*
> Empty the air and cold
> Empty the hour and long . . . .

Again and again the poems of this second collection narrate the tragedy of loss. 'Earth Does at length', for example, suggests that a return to the natural world helps to restore 'The wild lost city of a mother's love.' In 'Returned Soldier', through 'dreams deeper than El Alamein / A buried childhood stirs . . . .' to torment or console the protagonist waking to brute reality, 'the midnight rafters and the rain.' 'The Castle', 'Sea Noon', 'Evening Ode' and 'Tunnel Beach' have related elements, but of all the poems in this volume it is 'The Bay' which evokes the most tragic expression of loss:

.   .   .   .

So now I remember the bay, and the little spiders
On driftwood, so poisonous and quick.
The carved cliffs and the great outcrying surf
With currents round the rocks and the birds rising.
A thousand times an hour is torn across
And burned for the sake of going on living.
But I remember the bay that never was
And stand like stone, and cannot turn away.

What has caused this loss? It has been suggested that Baxter 'rests his poetry on the failure of what he conceives to be a natural conjunction; the 'promise of prodigious noon: / Childhood and age in one green cradle joined.'[1] The answer is an exact one in a negative sense, for it is the force of reality that Baxter laments here. Childhood had promised something other than 'the midnight rafters and the rain.' The illusion of Eden had become the nightmare reality. It was precisely because his expectations were unfulfilled that Baxter found himself living 'at maelstrom centre'.

The poems of *The Fallen House* repeat the theme. The second stanza of 'Autumn Waking', for example, mythologises the 'black swamp' of adolescent and adult miseries. The poem closes with a serene lyric passage which recalls

. . . another morning and another sun,
Myself a child high in the milk-cart riding,
Odour of fresh dung at the horse's heels
And calm daybreak upon the sea horizon.

The poem, too strained in the earlier part, is almost redeemed by the magnificent movement of this last section with its subdued presentation of the visual image.

'Temple Basin' also describes those earlier years 'when Sorrow was a child' which existed before 'Time slew the first Adam / In me.', yet because of its more extreme Wordsworthian pastoral romanticism this poem is less appealing than 'The Bay'.

'Victoria Lake' is in the same tradition. It records that idyllic mood in which 'a child walked and wondered / At the leaves' treasure house' who now in adulthood 'lies dumb, the black tongue dry / And the eyes weighed with coins . . . .'

In 'Poem by the Clock Tower, Sumner' he was still searching for

> *. . . the white stone that shall transmute*
> *Our average day to gold . . .*
> *The green lane that leads to the wishing well*
> *The secret house the fertile wilderness*
> *Where grief and memory are reconciled . . . .*

Yet there is hope, for he knows 'In heart of lethargy a drowned sun rising . . . .' The poem suggests that the problem of loss is partly countered by Christian revelation, by the illumination and indwelling of the Spirit, by our recognition of the patristic paradox that 'there can be no light without a Cross' and by our realisation that the only Eden lies in the future. This, the 'Christian track', is one of the three stratagems which Chapman has found Baxter employing as a counter to loss.

A further stratagem which he diagnosed is one 'of stoic recognition and resignation which [Baxter] bows to in Hardy.'[2] The critic referred to 'Wild Bees', a poem in which the mythological and the real are held in perfect balance, while the long cadences are a fine vehicle for the elegiac narrative and the high gravity of the conclusion:

.   .   .   .

> *But loss is a precious stone to me, a nectar*
> *Distilled in time, preaching the truth of winter*
> *To the fallen heart that does not cease to fall.*

He then went on to interpret these lines: 'We do what we must and what is finest in us, we give love, and the way the world is jointed causes us to work not good thus, but ill. It is, of course, a way of seeing Original Sin . . . .'[3]

While it is clear that the lines say something about the effects of the Fall, they certainly do not imply determinism. Loss is precious because it reminds us of our fallibility and thus drives us on to search for that 'green inn / Where life and death begin.' In Baxter's verse the imagery of the Fall is very often a vehicle for paradoxes.

'The Not-Yet-Made' from *In Fires of No Return* develops even further this theme of loss. In the first three verses of the poem Baxter describes children at play. They do not suspect the over-shadowing of a 'handsized cloud in the clear sky . . . .':

.   .   .   .

> *Can they interpret our graffiti saying—*

> I warn you of King Coffin;
> Avoid the ogress, who is lame . . . .

It is not that we who have departed that 'bright, relinquished kingdom' have gained happiness by the simple process of aging, but that ours is a different kind of serenity based on the acceptance of what is:

.   .   .   .

> *Not happiness its meaning,*
> *White stone of manhood gained*

Wrestling with the demon of the rock.
Without envy and observant,
Walk the bright, relinquished kingdom
Where summer burns and fades: listen
To the voice of noon on a wide shore,
Your peace not theirs, yet both held
In the hollow of a heart beating.

The diamond cutting-edge of much of Baxter's best verse has come from his painful awareness of Loss. No one else in our literature has manipulated this theme quite as effectively. In the early poems it was a lament for the lost innocence of childhood. But to stay still is to die, spiritually, aesthetically, and critics have been slow to recognise the energetic movement which has marked this development in his verse. The Oxford collections clarify the later, more positive, movement:

One learns acceptance from the dead:

To scrape the bones of the dead, how needful
Lest they should walk, undo forgetfulness[4] . . . .

from an awareness of transience:

And this, the moment of art, can never stay[5] . . . .

from suffering:

And when I made a mother of the keg
The town split open like an owl's egg
Breaking the ladders down. It was
Perhaps the winter of beginning[6] . . . .

from nature:

The slow language of the waves
Gave hope of truth to come[7] . . . .

If the strength of so many early poems came from the poignant expression of lost innocence symbolised by a mythical Eden ('But I remember the bay that never was / And stand like stone and cannot turn away.'), the subsequent course of Baxter's life seems to have led to an acceptance of what is. The realisation that there is no earthly Eden for adult or child has brought him peace of a kind:

.   .   .   .

> *As one who has buried his dead,*
> *Able at last to give with an open hand.*[8]

The strength of these later poems still comes, in part, from the contrast of *then* and *now,* but the note of grief is sounded less sharply. In its place one finds a new hardness of language, a wisdom learned painfully, and a clear, exact description of the natural scene similar to that of a Brasch poem, but charged with a greater energy.

In his latest work this shift has continued. The tragic awareness of loss has given way to a recognition of the need to accept reality, as 'The Bridge' implies:

> *Far up the creek I*
> *often rode in*
> *a rented canoe, my*
> *paddles barely touching*
> *the water's pollen dusted skin*
> *where gorse-pods floated,*
> *and slid under*
> *the Black Bridge's rusted*
> *bolts and tarry roof: there*
> *one could make sherbert from water*
> *with a matchbox full*
> *of fizzing fine*
> *powder. It tasted well*
> *nipping the tongue, in high*
> *summer, when crickets chirred at noon*
> *on each bush—lately*

LOSS AND THE SEARCH FOR EDEN

> *I went that way*
> *not thinking, and saw the*
> *bridge under fifty bull-*
> *dozed yards of gravel and dry clay.*[9]

This is the setting of the tragic action of 'Wild Bees', yet the movement of the poem is now un-romanticised, matter-of-fact. Baxter has learned to walk through the childhood garden 'without envy'.

In *Pig Island Letters* there occurs a poem which almost closes the casebook entry of Baxter's search for a childhood Eden. In the eleventh section of the 'Pig Island Letters' sequence he has described his relationship with his son who 'hands me easily / The key of entry' to the joys of childhood. But the father cannot enter because 'the journey has begun / Into the land where the sun is silent . . . .'

In the first section of the same sequence Baxter had written 'Man is a walking grave, / That is where I start from . . . .' Such an opinion is at extreme remove from the 'promise of prodigious noon'.

The elegiac note is sounded in poem after poem in this collection: in 'The Watch', 'East Coast Journey', 'Waipatiki Beach', 'At Taieri Mouth', 'At Rotorua', 'The Hollow Place', and in most of the narrative pieces as well.

In the free metrics he uses in so many of his late poems Baxter records his final position:

> *. . . As a man*
> *Grows older he does not want beer, bread, or the*
> *prancing flesh,*
> *But the arms of the eater of life, Hine-nui-te-po,*
>
> *With teeth of obsidian and hair like kelp*
> *Flashing and glimmering at the edge of the horizon.*[10]

In the course of his search for Eden Baxter had begun by looking for childhood and innocence. He has ended by embracing adulthood and the prospect of death.

THE POETRY OF JAMES K. BAXTER

It may be observed that on some occasions Baxter appears to regret the fact of death. The hesitation does not seem to occur because of self-regard but because it injures that *fraternitas* which is so prominent a feature of his writing. The opening poem in his first published volume is a lament that death has taken away 'The First Forgotten'. Perhaps the very best of the poems of loss written during Baxter's middle period is likewise concerned with this theme. 'The Fallen House' is engraved like an epitaph at the end of the volume of that name. A few ragged thistles grew where an old house once stood:

. . . .

It was not Woe that flaunted
Funereal plume and banner there,
Nor an Atridean doom that daunted
The heart with a lidless gorgon stare;
But darker the cradling bluegums, sombre the air,
By the wraith of dead joy haunted.

There once the murk was cloven
By hearthlight fondly flaring within:
Adamant seemed their hope and haven.
O Time, Time takes in a gin
The quick of being! Pale now and gossamer-thin
The web their lives had woven.

In the grand manner, with a resonance that owes something to Hardy, in a passage of grave archaic elegance, he lamented even then the breaking of the tribe.

Baxter's search for the lost happiness and innocence of a childhood Eden has given rise to a paradox: he sought life and found death. Of his writing he has said:

There is a spot in the arena to which the fighting
bull returns . . . and from which he comes out

more assured and formidable. For me it was once the beaches of the place I grew up in; then the pub; and latterly perhaps the hour of death which one looks forward to. If this spot is correctly located one can generally go on writing.[11]

In correctly locating this centre, Baxter's writing has gained a new assurance, a formidable maturity.

THE GROWTH OF STYLE

The style of Baxter's poems has altered considerably over the years. This has depended to some extent on his current models, for he has always been an imitative poet. Curnow noted this in his review of *Blow, Wind of Fruitfulness* when he remarked that Baxter 'writes like the true descendant of many poets . . . .'[1]

The habit of literary imitation has special dangers for a poet with the easy eloquence of Baxter. He has come to recognise this:

> *The problem for me in the '40s and '50s was to get rid of the mere echo language in my poems, the twists of phrase (and so of thought also) that belonged by right to Hardy or Yeats or Dylan Thomas or Louis MacNeice . . . not a bad thing in itself . . . but the habit is dangerous when the experience behind one's own poem is weak and trivial[2]. . . .*

Three degrees of imitation seem possible: structural imitation, imitation of structure and mood, and a comprehensive imitation of structure, mood and theme. All three are found at various stages in Baxter's work. (In fact, Baxter's talent for imitation has allowed him to publish a collection of skilful parodies of New Zealand poets in *The Iron Breadboard.*)

After the Romantic poets who influenced his adolescence, Baxter's next master was Hardy. In his writing Baxter discovered a congenial melancholy and the formal care of a good craftsman. The determinism built into poems like 'Thrushes', and the grave, archaic manner of 'The Fallen House' show this discipleship most plainly, but the under-current of pessimism which flows through 'Rocket Show', 'The Bay' and 'Sea Noon' also has its affinities in the work of the older writer.

The influence of Yeats on Baxter's writing has not been entirely beneficial. Baxter has undoubtedly recognised this, for he has never republished the later poems in *The Fallen House*—'Song for an Old Soak', 'The Immortals', 'The Glass Door' and 'Defence of Romantic Love'. In these poems the debt to Yeats was one of structure, mood and theme, and the personal voice was lost in the accents and technique of the model. It seems as if Baxter, the romantic-realist, was never able to assimilate the high resonance of the arch-priest of modern Romanticism without sounding phoney. This is simply another way of pointing to the dangers inherent in the vatic utterance. The tendency of *The Fallen House* was towards a high rhetoric, effective enough when the impetus behind the poem was a precise one, but portentous when this was vague.

In a review of MacNeice's *Collected Poems* Baxter has paid tribute to the Englishman's 'steady humanist affirmation in the face of war, betrayals, self-betrayal, bureaucratic monotony, the assaults of meaninglessness, the decay of romantic love—in a word, the ills of man[3]. . . .' We can thus identify a contributory influence to Baxter's own emphasis on the middle ground of existence, his concern for social minutiae, his use of detail, his anti-romantic and satiric modes and his wistful sensibility. More-over, Baxter has disclosed that the stanza form of 'Wild Bees' was borrowed from MacNeice. Although the poem relies in part on 'Street Scene', it is still only a way of handling themes that has been borrowed: Baxter's poem remains successful because it is founded in a genuine poetic impulse and strongly rooted in reality.

Baxter's contribution to *Poems Unpleasant* (1952) included a number of narrative and dramatic poems which represented a new direction in his writing. 'The Surfman's Story', for instance, indicates the astonishing ease with which Baxter adopts a new stanza form:

> *On such a day as this*
> *When breakers bay on the reef like a minutegun*
> *Or up the tall beach grind and hiss*
> *Like flattened snakes—we hauled out*
> *Tackle and lifeline, at the run,*
> *For two swept seaward, bathers, caught in the*
> *current's rout. . . .*

It also reveals his gift for the definitive image:

> .   .   .   .

> *Well—he was washed ashore*
> *Some weeks after, eaten by fishes, foul*
> *With tangleweed. She cried no more.*
> *We were married within the year—that house*
> *By the river's ours, with the climbing cowl*
> *Of woodsmoke, the paddock behind, in a nest of*
> *orchard boughs.*

Poems such as 'Conversation in a Road', 'Thoughts of a Dying Calvinist' and 'Lot' are successful experiments in a new mode and look forward to the later ballads, narrative and dramatic poems which he has written so well. 'Tarras Moon', 'Jack the Swagger's Song', 'Perseus', 'The Journey', 'Brown Bone', 'The Ballad of John Silent' and 'The First Communions' are fine examples of this kind of writing.

It has been suggested that a number of the later poems from *In Fires of No Return* are really a kind of self-communion. 'Letter to the World' is such a one; it is dense, allusive, and loses control over its multiple images. In these poems the compromise between what has to be said and the manner of saying it falters, and under the stress of vehement utterance the poetry tends to lose coherence. Even here, however, in this verse of unpuritanical introspection, there are the beginnings of a movement towards the later honest examination of reality which characterizes *Pig Island Letters*.

The new poems of *Howrah Bridge* owe much to Lawrence Durrell, and parts of *Pig Island Letters*, too, have sprung from this literary seeding-ground. 'At Rotorua', for instance, exemplifies the 'carped, carved, little two-lined stanzas' which Louis Johnson identified as part of Baxter's debt to Durrell.[4]

Of this allegiance Baxter has remarked: 'Durrell loosens up the chains of association, helping me to avoid heavy aphorisms about Time or God, and to keep the eye on the invaluable sensory image[5]. . . .' Baxter's reading of Durrell has coincided with his exorcism of emotional excesses and the inflated rhetoric which critics have censured in the past. Its positive contribution has been a sinewy verse bonded in the natural scene.

Robert Lowell's influence is, perhaps, the most recent. He has helped Baxter 'to use words as a straight-jacket to contain the violent experiences of the manic-depressive cycle[6]. . . .' Poems such as 'Thoughts of a Remuera Housewife', 'Great Uncles and Great-Aunts' and 'Henley Pub' have been described by Baxter as 'formal rhetoric with full rhymes and references to Greek mythology . . . to deal with the experiences of those who habitually embrace red-hot stoves[7] . . .' If in some of these poems Baxter loses imaginative control over the underlying myth ('Henley Pub'), or comes too close to his model ('Guy Fawkes Night'), in others, as in 'To a Print of Queen Victoria' or 'Tomcat', the poet's powerful perception, metrical control and deft use of half-rhymes fuse the poems into moving allegories of the human condition.

On occasions, more especially when it is influenced by Yeats or Lowell, Baxter's poetry is overwhelmed by its sources, but at its best this literary eclecticism has enriched his verse and given it a genuine universality of reference.

Although Baxter's remarkable technical expertise has allowed him to use a considerable number of verse forms, in general, since *The Fallen House,* his work has shown a progressive loosening of stanza and line. Such a freedom exists even within the syllabic poems of *Pig Island Letters.* Though some may regret this change from stricter forms, it is probable that this as much as anything has helped free his verse from the bonds of rhetoric.

Over the years his language has undergone considerable change. In *Beyond the Palisade* it was often diffuse, semi-private. In *Blow, Wind of Fruitfulness* and *The Fallen House* it moved between the gravely resonant and the inflections of common speech as in 'Elegy for an Unknown Soldier' or 'The Morgue':

.   .   .   .

But when at length, with stiff broom and bucket
I opened the door wide—well, there was nothing
To fear: only the bare close concrete wall,
A slab of stone, and a wheeled canvas stretcher,
For Death had shifted house to his true home
And mansion, ruinous, of the human heart.

In the late 'fifties when his language sometimes became melodramatic, he was still able to write that triumph of colloquialism, 'Lament for Barney

Flanagan'. The best of Baxter's poems of the 'sixties give the illusion of spoken language without the carelessness of speech.

Sometimes Baxter uses a solely discursive mode of writing in contrast to the imagistic method used in a poem like 'The Bay', and in general he employs statement more frequently than implication, but he also utilises natural objects as symbols to an extent which critics have failed to recognise. At the same time, he possesses an image-making faculty unrivalled by any other New Zealand poet and on occasions his imagery has that Orphic power which gives the poetry an overwhelming significance as in the conclusion of 'Rocket Show':

.   .   .   .

It is the rain streaming reminds me of
Those ardent showers, cathartic love and grief.
As I walked home through the cold streets by moon-
    light,
My steps ringing in the October night,
I thought of our strange lives, the grinding cycle
Of death and renewal come to full circle,
And of man's heart, that blind Rosetta stone,
Mad as the polar moon, decipherable by none.[8]

During the last fifteen years some critics have doubted that Baxter has fulfilled his promise. It is true that he has not always been sufficiently selective about what he has published, but it may also be that there are some who have already formed their opinions about what is 'genuine Baxter' and who then regret his movement away from a position their own expectations had prescribed. This is to mis-understand the general movement of his life and work.

Baxter has written a large number of very good poems. What is more notable is that his verse has continued to gain strength as he has fought the difficult battle of moral and literary detachment. He is, in fact, much more than just a New Zealand poet. The price he has paid has been one of total commitment to those things that really seem to matter. He has had to look into the dark mirror. From it he has brought back a sombre vision of reality, a sensitive presentation of spiritual states and a unifying power of the imagination. When these are sustained by 'a controlled use of language the result is a heightened, liberated personality and a verse more memorable than any other in our literature.

It is probable, however, that such a growth to poetic maturity concerns him less than the urge to continue the search for spiritual adulthood—a search he outlined as a twenty-two-year-old student at Canterbury University:

. . . .

> *Jesus and Mary, make*
> *The springtime come again*
> *Somewhere sometime, or take*
> *The burden of my pain.*
> *I seek the green inn*
> *Where life and death begin.*[9]

C. K. Stead has written about what matters in poetry: 'The human personality transmuted into poetry, or transmitted through it, is what matters—its magnitude, its strength, its capacity to suffer and affirm the common range of experience, and to lose itself there[10]. . . .' The passage could well serve as an epigraph to the poetry of James K. Baxter.

PUBLICATIONS BY JAMES K. BAXTER

Beyond the Palisade (poems); Caxton Press, Christchurch; 1944.

Blow, Wind of Fruitfulness (poems); Caxton; 1948.

Recent Trends in New Zealand Poetry (criticism); Caxton; 1951.

Poems Unpleasant (with Louis Johnson and Anton Vogt); Pegasus Press, Christchurch; 1952.

The Fallen House (poems); Caxton; 1953.

Traveller's Litany (a poem); Handcraft Press, Wellington; 1955.

The Fire and the Anvil (some notes on modern poetry); New Zealand University Press, Wellington; 1955.

The Iron Breadboard (verse parodies); Mermaid Press, Wellington; 1957.

The Night Shift (poems: with Charles Doyle, Louis Johnson and Kendrick Smithyman); Capricorn Press, Wellington; 1957.

In Fires of No Return (selected poems); Oxford University Press; 1958.

Chosen Poems; Konkan Institute of the Arts and Sciences (for private circulation); 1958.

Two Plays; Capricorn Press, Wellington; 1959.

Howrah Bridge and other poems; Oxford; 1961.

New Zealand in Colour (photographs by Kenneth and Jean Bigwood; text by Baxter); Reed, Wellington; 1961.

Poems: Poetry Magazine; Teachers' College, Wellington; 1964.

Pig Island Letters (poems); Oxford; 1966.
Aspects of Poetry in New Zealand (criticism); Caxton; 1967.

The Lion Skin (poems); the Bibliography Room, University of Otago; 1967.

The Man on the Horse (lectures and autobiographical articles); University of Otago Press; 1967.

The Flowering Cross (pastoral articles); The Tablet Press, Dunedin; 1969.

The Rock Woman (selected poems); Oxford; 1969.

REFERENCES

BIOGRAPHICAL

1. 'Notes on the Education of a New Zealand Poet';
   The Man on the Horse; p. 122.
2. Biographical note on Baxter in the *Penguin Book of
   New Zealand Verse* (edited by Allen Curnow; 1960)
   p. 313.
3. 'Notes . . .' l.c.
4. ibid. p. 124.
5. 'The Hollow Place'; *Pig Island Letters;* p. 31.
6. *The Fallen House;* p. 18.
7. ibid. p. 19.
8. ibid. p. 20.
9. 'Notes . . .' l.c. p. 133.
10. 'School Days'; *New Zealand Poetry Yearbook,* Vol. 9
    (1960) p. 23.
11. 'Letter to Noel Ginn'; *Beyond the Palisade;* p. 38.
12-17. 'Notes . . .' l.c.
18. *New Zealand Poetry Yearbook,* Vol. 9 (1960) p. 27.
19. *Pig Island Letters;* p. 41.
20. 'Essay on the Higher Learning'; *Spike* (Victoria
    University) 1961, p. 62.
21. ibid.
22. Letter to the author 29 March 1961.
23. 'Notes . . .' l.c. p. 121.

POETRY AS MYTH

1. 'Notes . . .' l.c. p. 122.
2. ibid.
3. Letter to the author 8 July 1961.
4. 'Conversation with an Ancestor'; *The Man on the
   Horse;* p. 23.

5. *Poems Unpleasant;* p. 21.
6. *The Fallen House;* p. 23.
7. *Landfall;* March 1959; p. 88.

THE SEARCH FOR ORDER IN NATURE

1. *A Book of New Zealand Verse 1923-45;* Caxton (1945) p. 52.
2. Introduction to the *Penguin Book of New Zealand Verse;* p 21.
3. ibid. p. 62.
4. 'The Hollow Place'; *Pig Island Letters;* p. 31.
5. 'Death of a Man'; *Beyond the Palisade;* p. 15.
6. 'Earth Does at Length'; *Blow, Wind of Fruitfulness;* p. 21.
7. *Recent Trends in New Zealand Poetry;* p. 18.
8. *The Rock Woman;* p. 83.
9. 'The River'; New Zealand *Listener;* 14 October 1966.

THE SEARCH FOR ORDER THROUGH LOVE

1. *Beyond the Palisade;* p. 39.
2. ibid. p. 28.
3. 'Letter to Noel Ginn 11'; *Blow, Wind of Fruitfulness;* p. 42.
4. 'Mr Baxter's Progress'; Joan Steven's review of *Howrah Bridge;* New Zealand *Listener;* 18 May 1962.
5. Robert Chapman in *Landfall;* September 1953, p. 209.
6. 'My Love Late Walking'; *In Fires of No Return;* p. 55.
7. *Landfall;* June 1958; p. 184.
8. Undated letter to the author.
9. *Landfall;* March 1959; p. 85.
10. 'Night in Delhi'; *Howrah Bridge;* p. 34.
11. Undated letter to the author.
12. Section 3 of title poem; *Pig Island Letters* p. 5.
13. 'The Virgin and the Temptress'; *The Man on the Horse;* p. 81.
14. 'Notes . . .'; *The Man on the Horse;* p. 153.
15. New Zealand *Listener;* 15 December 1967.
16. Section 6 of title poem; *Pig Island Letters;* p. 8.

THE SEARCH FOR ORDER THROUGH RELIGION

1. 'Cry Mourn'; *Beyond the Palisade;* p. 12.
2. *The Fallen House;* p. 25.
3. 'To God the Son'; *In Fires of No Return;* p. 47.
4. New Zealand *Listener;* 17 April 1959.
5. Letter to the author; 17 November 1961.
6. *Hilltop;* 1: 2, p. 6; June 1949.
7. *Howrah Bridge;* p. 56.

THE SEARCH FOR ORDER IN SOCIETY

1. *Recent Trends in New Zealand Poetry;* p. 18.
2. Letter to the author; 10 December 1962.
3. ibid. 26 April 1963.
4. *In Fires of No Return;* p. 66.
5. *Howrah Bridge;* p. 36.
6. 'The Sixties'; *Howrah Bridge;* p. 55.
7. New Zealand *Listener;* 8 December 1967.
8. 'At Rotorua'; *Pig Island Letters;* p. 28.
9. 'Notes. . .' p. 129 (The next four quotations are from the same source).
10. 'Letter to Noel Ginn 11'; *Blow, Wind of Fruitfulness;* p. 43.
11. New Zealand *Poetry Yearbook,* Vol. 10 (1961-62) p. 26.
12. 'Conversation with an Ancestor'; *The Man on the Horse;* p. 14.
13. Title article; *The Man on the Horse;* pp. 93-4.
14. 'Notes . . .'; l.c. p. 137.
15. Broadsheet published by John Summers, Christchurch, N.Z. [1968].
16. 'On Reading Yevtushenko'; *The Rock Woman;* p. 81.

THE POETRY OF LOSS AND THE SEARCH FOR EDEN

1. *Landfall;* September 1953 p. 212.
2. ibid.
3. ibid.
4. 'At Hokianga'; *The Rock Woman;* p. 29.
5. Section 1 of title poem; *Pig Island Letters;* p. 3.
6. Section 3. ibid. p. 5.

7. 'The Waves'; *The Rock Woman;* p. 84.
8. 'New Zealand'; *The Rock Woman;* p. 80.
9. New Zealand *Listener;* 10 March 1967.
10. 'East Coast Journey'; *Pig Island Letters;* p. 24.
11. Introductory article to his poems in *Recent Poetry in New Zealand* (ed. Charles Doyle); Collins (1965) p. 30.

THE GROWTH OF STYLE

1. *Landfall;* September 1948; p. 230.
2. *Recent Poetry in New Zealand;* p. 29.
3. New Zealand *Listener;* 14 July 1967.
4. Editorial to New Zealand *Poetry Yearbook* '64, Vol. 11; p. 12.
5. *Recent Poetry in New Zealand.* l.c.
6. ibid. p. 30.
7. ibid.
8. *The Fallen House;* p. 22.
9. 'Song for an Old Soak'; ibid. p. 25.
10. 'Fairburn'; *Landfall;* December 1966; p. 381.